FASHION DOG

Thirty designs to knit, crochet and sew

First published in Great Britain 2010 by Search Press Limited,
Wellwood, North Farm Road, Tunbridge Wells, Kent TN2 3DR

Original title: Fashion Dog

© 2009 by Editions Marie Claire – Société d'Information et de Créations (SIC)

English translation by Cicero Translations

English edition edited and typeset by GreenGate Publishing Services

ISBN: 978-1-84448-608-3

Knitting design: Marie-Noëlle Bayard and Marguerite Aténian
Sewing design: Catherine Charapoff
Photography: Pierre Nicou
Instructions: Marguerite Aténian
Diagrams and charts: Olivier Ribaillier
Graphic design, layout: Either Studio

Publishers' Note:
For knitting needles and crochet hooks, both metric and US sizes are given. Similarly, both UK and US crochet terms are provided; the UK term first, followed by the US term. For clarity, the US term is italicised and placed in brackets.

FASHION DOG

Thirty designs to knit, crochet and sew

Contents

Projects

Knitting and crochet designs

Sewing designs

Accessories

Coats and accessories to knit and transform
our favourite little companions into 'fashion dogs'.

Snug
chic

Sportswear for Toby

Complete with hood and zip, this jogging-style top knitted in stocking stitch is perfect for a sporty dog. A shoulder pocket adds that little something extra.
Instructions on page 68.

Cleo loves her Irish knit sweater

Featuring a chic front-zip opening plus a smart cabled back and collar, this sleeveless sweater would look adorable on any small dog.
Instructions on page 71.

Smart Bailey

With its unusual feature belt and graphic two-coloured Fair-isle design, this smart coat is particularly becoming on dogs with long bodies like the dachshund.
Instructions on page 74.

Ecru sweater for Caramel

Knitted in rib stitch with a long cable along the back, this simple, comfortable roll-neck sweater suits all our little companions.
Instructions on page 77.

Star act

Ideal for muscly dogs like Toto, this coat is easier to make than it looks – the letters are added with Swiss darning (duplicate stitch) and the stars are buttons. *Instructions on page 80.*

Bad-boy vest

Give your dog some street cred with this smart vest, which features a jewelled skull and crossbones on the back.
Instructions on page 83.

Floral fancy

This very feminine coat, like a dress, is knitted in rib stitching and decorated with silver crocheted flowers.
Instructions on page 87.

Pretty in pink

With its bright colour and fancy neckline, this original coat is knitted in star
and chevron stitch to guarantee that your dog gets noticed.
Instructions on page 90.

Cleo all in grey

Knitted in striped stocking stitch, this coat has a high neck and three-quarter length sleeves. A fashionable look for small urban dogs.
Instructions on page 93.

Top dog Bailey

This is an easy-knit coat for fashionista dogs worked entirely in garter stitch
(knit every row).
Instructions on page 95.

Lovely, all at sea

For weekends by the sea, this is a smart nautical outfit in navy and white with gold buttons on the shoulders.
Instructions on page 97.

Couture wear for Toto

Knitted in diamond stitch and decorated with gold studs,
this is a chic coat for special occasions.
Instructions on page 99.

Short scarf for Caramel

Worn like a collar, this scarf is knitted in stocking stitch
with a slip-stitch design in two colours.
Instructions on page 101.

14 Long scarf

This soft cabled scarf is so smart that you'll want one for yourself.
Instructions on page 102.

15 Leg warmers

These leg warmers feature the same cable design to match the scarf.
Instructions on page 102.

Seventies style for Lovely

Here's a patchwork rug made of joined, crocheted squares to throw over a cushion or put in her basket.
Instructions on page 103.

Floral scarf for Lovely

A scarf for the first frosts, made from hexagonal rosettes, crocheted and joined together.
Instructions on page 106.

Royal cushion for Bella

This chunky, tasselled, Aran-style cushion is knitted in soft, easy-care yarn so that your dog can sleep like a little princess.
Instructions on page 109.

Classic, elegant outfits to protect your dog
against the wind and rain.

19 Pablo loves the rain

A cotton-lined sou'wester for walking in comfort whatever the weather.
A very practical garment for our four-legged friends.
Instructions on page 111.

20 Twice as nice reversible coat

Entirely reversible, this two-in-one cotton coat can be worn on the gingham or polka-dot side depending on the day and the walk.
Instructions on page 113.

Charlie lords it up

The same pattern as on page 44, but Scottish style. The coat is lined with flannelette for warmth and comfort.
Instructions on page 114.

So chic

A rug for a sofa, chair, a pouffe or the floor. Both decorative and comfortable, dogs will love sleeping on it.
Instructions on page 116.

A couture-style collar and lead and fun lucky pendants –
irresistible accessories for our little friends.

Dog
attitude

Haute couture collar for Tinker

An elegant collar to make and sew, covered in fabric and decorated with a jewel.
Instructions on page 118.

Haute couture
24 lead

A fabric lead with gold
trigger hook to match
the collar.
Instructions on page 118.

Jewelled collar for Charlie

Beads, scooby strings, ribbons, bells, a heart and medals attached using rings
and trigger hooks – a collar for celebrations (not to be worn unsupervised).
Instructions on page 120.

26 Skull and crossbones pendant for Clovis

Fun and offbeat, these pendants are crocheted in black or white with contrasting embroidered details and can be worn together or separately.
Instructions on page 121.

Bone pendant

These little bones are made of very soft cotton and can be attached to your dog's collar with trigger hooks.
Instructions on page 122.

Precious pendant for Pablo

Like a jewel, this refined bone pendant is crocheted in silver yarn to decorate his collar.
Instructions on page 122.

Little bells for Lovely

Crocheted orange, red and yellow bells for decorating her collar.
Instructions on page 123.

30

A heart for Bella

A crocheted heart with embroidered letters.
A delightful pendant for a delightful little dog.
Instructions on page 124.

Instructions

Tips and tricks

Take measurements

- To make the designs, **carefully measure** your dog:
  collar size, chest size, back length and, sometimes, paw height.
- The **back** is measured from the base of the neck to the tail.
- The **chest size** is measured right in the middle of the abdomen.
- In the designs to knit, the size indicates **the dimensions of the coat** made each time.

For the sewn designs

- For **the fabric and oilskin coats**, take the dimensions of your dog very precisely.
- We supply a single pattern for the three sewn designs. You will need **to adapt this pattern** to the dimensions of your dog.
- **Choose washable fabrics**; you will be able to wash the coat in a machine at 30°C.
- **Avoid fabrics** which itch or are too fluffy.
- Before sewing, **wash** all the fabrics and flannelette that you are going to use to soften and preshrink it.
- **Adhesive Velcro** makes it easier to dress your dog but it must be sewn on as it may become detached with washing.
- **Zigzag stitch** enables all the layers of fabric to be held together.

To increase the size of a design

• All **the knitted coats** in this book are **very stretchy**.
You can make them as they are even if the collar or chest size of your dog differs by a few centimetres from the dimensions shown. However, if there is a significant difference, add more stitches to the belly pattern according to the design:

    • **For coats 1, 2, 10 and 12:** Add 4 stitches for another 2cm (¾in).

    • **For coats 4, 8, 9 and 11:** Add 6 stitches for another 2cm (¾in).

• **For coat 7:**
Add 8 stitches for another 2cm (¾in).

• **For coat 5:**
Add 2 stitches on each belly half for another 2cm (¾in) in total.

• **For coat 6:**
Add 3 stitches on each belly half for another 2cm (¾in) in total.

• **For coat 3:**
Knitted in a single piece, add 2 stitches at each end for another 2cm (¾in) in total and knit them in plain stocking stitch.

• **For the length**, add the required number of centimetres by increasing the number of rows (without decreasing or increasing the number of stitches) in the same way on the two parts (back and belly).

Sportswear for Toby

SIZE

Collar size 26cm (10¼in), chest size 39cm (15¼in), total back length 35cm (13¾in).

MATERIALS

Aran/worsted knitting yarn in an easy-care blend: three balls of grey, one ball of red • 10cm (4in) zip • 3.5mm/US 4 knitting needles or size needed to obtain the correct tension (see page 69).

Note: The '1' on the back is added at the end with Swiss darning.

STITCHES USED

Stocking stitch: *knit 1 row, purl 1 row*, repeat from * to *.
2/2 rib: *K2, P2*, repeat from * to *.
Striped bands: on a stocking-stitch background in grey, purl 2 rows on the right side in red, 4 rows in stocking stitch on the right side in grey and purl 2 rows on the right side in red.

Decrease 1 stitch, 2 stitches from each edge (on the right side of the work): work 1 stitch, then slip 1 stitch, knit 1 stitch and pass the slipped stitch over (slip1, K1, psso). Work the rest of the row until you are 2 stitches from the end then knit 2 stitches together (K2tog).
Increase 1 stitch on each side of the centre stitch (on the right side of the work): work until you are 1 stitch from the centre stitch then knit into the front and back of the next stitch (Kfb). Knit the centre stitch then knit into the front and back of the next stitch. Work to the end of the row.
Increase 1 stitch, 2 stitches from each edge (on the right side of the work): work 1 stitch then knit into the front and back of the next stitch. Work until you are 2 stitches from the end then knit into the front and back of the next stitch. Work the final stitch.
Increase 2 stitches, 2 stitches from each edge (on the right side of the work): work 1 stitch then knit into the front and back of the next 2 stitches. Work until you are 3 stitches from the end then knit into the front and back of the next 2 stitches. Work the final stitch.

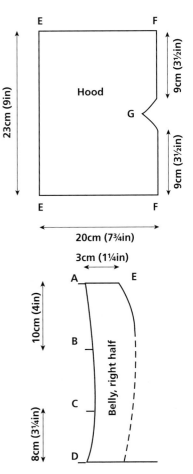

TENSION

A 10cm (4in) square in stocking stitch, using 3.5mm/US 4 needles = 19 stitches and 28 rows.

METHOD

Back: using grey cast on 21 stitches. Using 3.5mm/US 4 needles, work in stocking stitch, increasing at each end of every second row: *first 2 stitches, then 1 stitch*. Repeat 4 times from * to * to obtain 45 stitches. Work another 2 rows in grey stocking stitch and then make the striped band. When the piece measures 34cm (13½in), cast off all the stitches. With the grey yarn, pick up 54 stitches at the bottom of the back, knit 4 rows in 2/2 rib, beginning and ending with 2 knit stitches; cast off all the stitches.

Belly: cast on 21 stitches in grey using 3.5mm/US 4 needles and work in stocking stitch, increasing 1 stitch on each side of the centre stitch every sixth row, 4 times. Simultaneously decrease 1 stitch at each end every tenth row, 4 times. When the piece measures 17cm (6¾in), cast off the centre stitch and finish each half separately by decreasing 1 stitch on the inner side every sixth row, 4 times. When the piece measures 27cm (10¾in), cast off all the stitches.

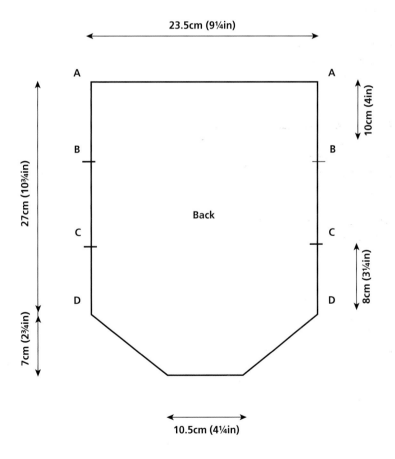

23.5cm (9¼in)

10cm (4in)

27cm (10¾in)

8cm (3¼in)

7cm (2¾in)

Back

A   A

B   B

C   C

D   D

10.5cm (4¼in)

– – – – – – – – = centre stitch

Sportswear for Toby (continued)

Hood: with grey cast on 39 stitches. Using 3.5mm/US 4 needles knit 4 rows in stocking stitch and then make the striped band. When the piece measures 9cm (3½in), decrease 1 stitch at the right end, every second row, 3 times. Then decrease 2 stitches on the next alternate row. Now start to increase: on the right end, every second row, increase 2 stitches the first time then 1 stitch 3 times. Work 9cm (3½in) straight, including the striped band as before, then cast off.

Pocket: cast on 16 stitches using 3.5mm/US 4 needles and knit 4 rows in 2/2 rib, beginning and ending with 3 knit stitches. Continue in stocking stitch for 2 rows, then make the band by knitting just 2 grey rows instead of 4 rows between the red rows. Continue with the grey yarn for 6 rows, then decrease 1 stitch, 2 stitches from the edges, every second row, 5 times. Pull the yarn through the 6 remaining stitches, tighten and knot.

Sleeve: cast on 38 stitches in grey using 3.5mm/US 4 needles and knit 6 rows in 2/2 rib, beginning and ending with 2 knit stitches. Continue in stocking stitch for 2 rows, then purl 2 rows with red and work 2 rows in stocking stitch with grey. Cast off all the stitches and knit a second sleeve.

JOINING AND FINISHING

Fold the hood right sides together, matching **F** to **F** and **E** to **E**. Sew the top of the hood from **G** to **F**. With the grey yarn, pick up 76 stitches on the edge of the hood from **E** to **E**, knit 6 rows in 2/2 rib, beginning and ending with 3 knit stitches and cast off all the stitches. Sew the belly to the back from **A** to **B** and from **C** to **D**.

Sew the sleeves to the armholes from **B** to **C**. Sew the hood around the neck hole from **E** to **E** passing by **A**. Sew in the zip. Place the pocket on the right shoulder, 2cm (¾in) from the neck and the tip of the pocket 1cm (½in) from the zip, and sew on with small stitches. Embroider the '1' using Swiss darning (duplicate stitch). Make a heart with the red yarn (see page 124). Fix on to the zip.

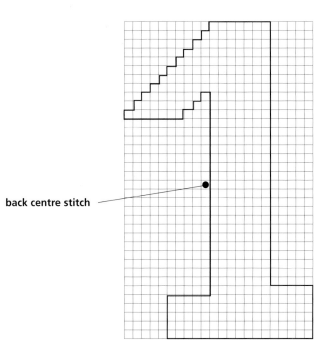

back centre stitch

Cleo loves her Irish knit sweater

SIZE

Collar size 24cm (9½in), chest size 34cm (13½in), total back length 28cm (11in).

MATERIALS

Double knitting/sportweight knitting yarn in an easy-care blend: two balls of olive • 4mm/US 6 knitting needles or size needed to obtain the correct tension (see opposite) • one stitch holder • one cable needle • 11cm (4¼in) zip.

STITCHES USED

Garter stitch: knit every row.
Garter diamonds and ribs: follow the diagram on page 73.
Raised cables: follow the diagram on page 72.
3 left cross stitches (K2 and P1): slip 2 stitches to a cable needle in front, purl the next stitch, then knit the 2 stitches from the cable needle.

3 right cross stitches (P1 and K2): slip 1 stitch to a cable needle at the back, knit the next 2 stitches, then purl the stitch from the cable needle.
4 left cross stitches (K2 and P2): slip 2 stitches to a cable needle in front, purl the next 2 stitches, then knit the 2 stitches from the cable needle.
4 right cross stitches (P2 and K2): slip 2 stitches to a cable needle at the back, knit the next 2 stitches, then purl the 2 stitches from the cable needle.
5 right cross stitches (K2, P1, K2): slip 3 stitches to a cable needle at the back, knit the next 2 stitches, put the third stitch from the cable needle back on to the left-hand needle, purl, passing behind the 2 stitches from the cable needle, then knit the 2 stitches from the cable needle.
Increase 1 stitch on each side of the centre stitch (on the right side of the work): work until you are 1 stitch from the centre stitch then knit into the front and back of the next stitch (Kfb). Knit the centre stitch then knit into the front and back of the next stitch. Work to the end of the row.

TENSION

One 10cm (4in) square of garter diamonds and ribs, using 4mm/US 6 needles = 20 stitches and 30 rows.

Cleo loves her Irish knit sweater (continued)

METHOD

Back: cast on 41 stitches using 4 mm/US 6 needles and knit 2 rows in garter stitch, then continue with diamonds and ribs following the charts on page 73. To centre the motif, knit 3 garter stitches, followed by 1 row of the diagram from stitch 5 to stitch 13 and 2 rows of the diagram from stitch 1 to stitch 13, ending with 3 garter stitches.

Belly: cast on 19 stitches using 4mm/US 6 needles and knit in garter stitch following the chart, increasing on each side of the centre stitch and 2 stitches from each edge as indicated on the chart. At point **S**, cast off the centre stitch and finish each half separately.

Neck band: cast on 18 stitches using 4mm/ US 6 needles and knit in raised cables. Work the first 2 stitches in garter stitch, then the next 2 stitches in reverse stocking stitch, followed by the 11 stitches in the diagram and finally 3 reverse stocking stitches.

Repeat the 14 rows in the diagram 5 times and cast off all the stitches.

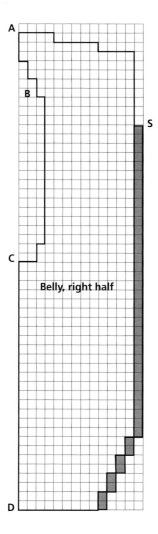

Belly, right half

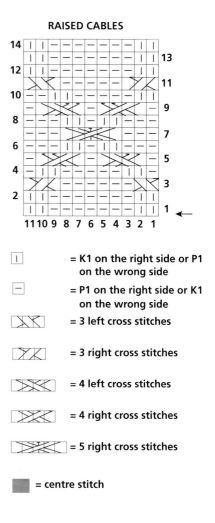

RAISED CABLES

	= K1 on the right side or P1 on the wrong side
	= P1 on the right side or K1 on the wrong side
	= 3 left cross stitches
	= 3 right cross stitches
	= 4 left cross stitches
	= 4 right cross stitches
	= 5 right cross stitches
	= centre stitch

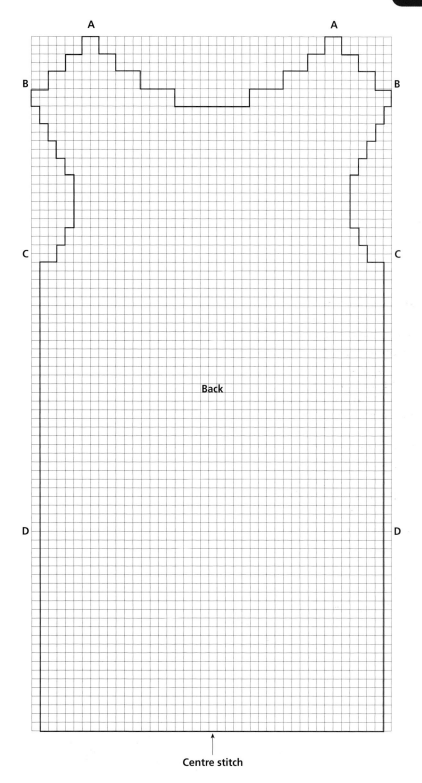

JOINING AND FINISHING

Sew the belly to the back from **A** to **B** and from **C** to **D**, gently stretching the garter stitch of the belly. Attach the neck band and then the zip.

DIAMONDS AND RIBS

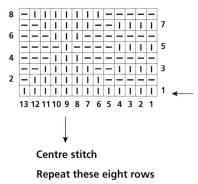

Centre stitch

Repeat these eight rows

Smart Bailey

SIZE

Collar size 26cm (10¼in), chest size 36cm (14¼in), total back length 45cm (17¾in).

MATERIALS

Aran/worsted knitting yarn in an easy-care blend: two balls of yellow, one ball of purple • 4mm/US 6 knitting needles or size to obtain the correct tension • two stitch holders • one belt buckle for a belt roughly 30mm wide.

STITCHES USED

Half fisherman's rib: number of stitches for symmetry: multiple of 4 + 1 + 1 edge stitch at each end. **Row 1** (right side of the work): 1 edge stitch, *K2, P1, K1*, repeat from * to *, end with K1 and 1 edge stitch. **Row 2:** 1 edge stitch, P1, *K3, P1*, repeat from * to * and end with 1 edge stitch. Repeat these 2 rows.

Fair-isle knitting: follow the diagram.

TENSIONS

One 10cm (4in) square in half fisherman's rib, using 4mm/US 6 needles = 27 stitches and 30 rows.

One 10cm (4in) square in Fair-isle knitting, using 4mm/US 6 needles = 20 stitches and 22 rows.

METHOD

In a single piece beginning with the neck: cast on 66 stitches in yellow using 4mm/US 6 needles and knit 10 rows in half fisherman's rib. In the next row, increase 1 stitch on the thirty-third stitch by knitting into the front and back of the stitch and continue in Fair-isle pattern. Make the centre stitch of the Fair-isle pattern the centre stitch of the work, i.e. begin with the tenth stitch of the Fair-isle pattern. At the twenty-third row of Fair-isle stitching, shape the armholes by working on the 47 centre stitches and leaving 10 stitches aside at each end. Knit in Fair-isle pattern for 20 rows and then leave these 47 stitches aside. Pick up the 10 stitches on the right and knit 20 rows, increasing 1 stitch on the right every fourth row twice. Leave aside the 12 stitches obtained and repeat in reverse, on the 10 stitches on the left. Pick up all 71 stitches. Decrease 1 stitch at each end, every fourth row, 4 times (63 stitches). When the piece measures 30cm (11¾in), cast off 11 stitches at each end and then decrease 1 stitch at the beginning of every sixth and seventh row, 6 times (29 stitches). When the piece measures 42cm (16½in), cast off all the stitches.

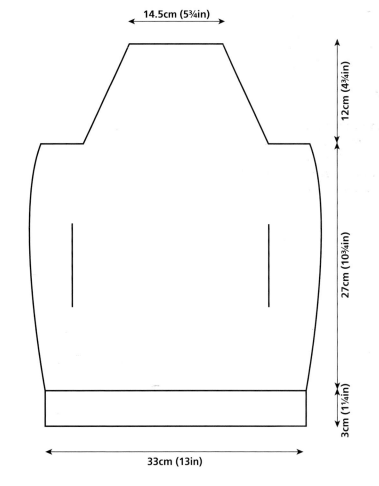

14.5cm (5¾in)

12cm (4¾in)

27cm (10¾in)

3cm (1¼in)

33cm (13in)

Smart Bailey (continued)

Armhole bands: cast on 46 stitches in purple yarn. Knit a few rows in stocking stitch then, continuing with yellow, purl 1 row on the wrong side, then knit 6 half fisherman's rib rows and cast off all the stitches. Knit a second armhole band.

Back edging: cast on 122 stitches in purple yarn. Knit a few rows in stocking stitch then, continuing with yellow, purl 1 row on the wrong side, then knit 6 rows in half fisherman's rib and cast off all the stitches.

Half belt: cast on 146 stitches in yellow and knit 8 rows in half fisherman's rib; cast off all the stitches.

JOINING AND FINISHING

Gently unravel the purple yarn of the back edging and armhole bands and sew the bands in place with backstitches. Join the belly. Fix the buckle on to the half belt and sew it with small stitches to the coat (see photo on page 74).

FAIR-ISLE PATTERN

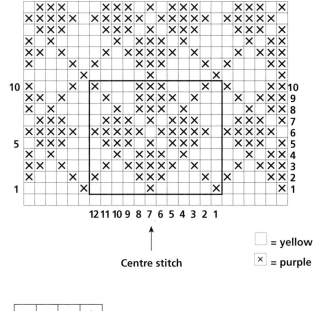

12 11 10 9 8 7 6 5 4 3 2 1

↑
Centre stitch

☐ = yellow

⊠ = purple

Repeat these two rows

Half fisherman's rib

⊡ = K1 on the right side or P1 on the wrong side

⊟ = P1 on the right side or K1 on the wrong side

Ecru sweater for Caramel

SIZE

Collar size 28cm (11in), chest size 36cm (14¼in), total back length 42cm (16½in).

MATERIALS

Aran/worsted knitting yarn in an easy-care blend: two balls of ecru • 3.5mm/US 4 knitting needles or size needed to obtain the correct tension (see page 78) • one cable needle.

STITCHES USED

1/1 rib: *K1, P1*, repeat from * to *.
2/2 rib: *K2, P2*, repeat from * to *.
Diamonds and cables: follow the diagram.
3 left cross stitches (K2 and P1): slip 2 stitches to a cable needle in front, purl the next stitch then knit the 2 stitches from the cable needle.

3 right cross stitches (P1 and K2): slip 1 stitch to a cable needle at the back, knit the next 2 stitches, then purl the stitch from the cable needle.

4 left cross stitches (K2 and K2): slip 2 stitches to a cable needle in front, knit the next 2 stitches, then knit the 2 stitches from the cable needle.

Increase 1 stitch on each side of the centre stitch (on the right side of the work): work until you are 1 stitch from the centre stitch then knit into the front and back of the next stitch (Kfb). Knit the centre stitch then knit into the front and back of the next stitch. Work to the end of the row.

Decrease 1 stitch on each side of the centre stitch (on the right side of the work): 2 stitches from the centre stitch, knit the 2 stitches together, knit the centre stitch, then knit the next 2 stitches together.

Ecru sweater for Caramel (continued)

TENSION

One 10cm (4in) square in 1/1 rib and cable stitch, using 3.5mm/US 4 needles = 24 stitches and 29 rows.

METHOD

Back: cast on 49 stitches using 3.5mm/US 4 needles and knit in 1/1 rib, increasing 1 stitch at each end, every second row, 10 times (69 stitches). At the same time, once the piece measures 2cm (¾in), increase 1 stitch on the centre stitch and begin a band of diamonds and cables on the 20 centre stitches. When the piece measures 33cm (13in), decrease 1 stitch at each end, every fourth row, 6 times (58 stitches). At the same time as the final end decrease, cast off the 28 centre stitches and finish each part separately, casting off 8 stitches from the neck side on the first row and the 7 remaining on the second row.

Belly: cast on 19 stitches using 3.5mm/US 4 needles and knit in 1/1 rib, beginning and ending with a knit stitch. When increasing and decreasing, maintain the knit stitch in the centre; depending on the number of stitches, you will sometimes have 2 purl stitches on each side of it. Increase 1 stitch on each side

of the centre stitch every fourth row, 6 times (31 stitches). When the piece measures 14cm (5½in), decrease 1 stitch on each side of the centre stitch every fourth row, 6 times. Cast off the remaining 19 stitches.

JOINING AND FINISHING

Sew the belly to the back from **A** to **B** on the right of the back. Pick up 70 stitches on the neck. Knit in 2/2 rib, beginning and ending with K2, for 11cm (4¼in) and cast off all the stitches. Carry out the second part of the sewing from **A** to **B**.

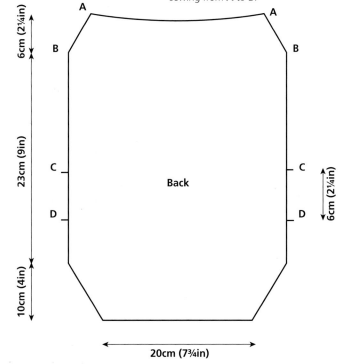

Pick up 42 stitches on the armholes from **C** to **C** passing through **B**. Knit in 2/2 rib, beginning and ending with K2, for 5cm (2in) and cast off all the stitches. Sew the sides and sleeves. Close the neck seam, reversing the seam halfway as the collar is worn folded.

– – – – = centre stitch

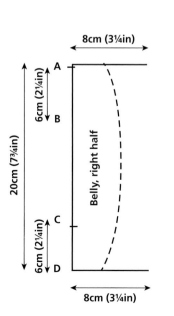

8cm (3¼in)

6cm (2¼in)

A

B

20cm (7¾in)

Belly, right half

6cm (2¼in)

C

D

8cm (3¼in)

DIAMONDS AND CABLES

| | = K1 on the right side or P1 on the wrong side

| – | = P1 on the right side or K1 on the wrong side

= 3 left cross stitches

= 3 right cross stitches

= 4 left cross stitches

Repeat from *to*

Star act

SIZE

Collar size 54cm (21¼in), chest size 66cm (26in), total back length 37cm (14½in).

MATERIALS

Aran/worsted knitting yarn in a wool blend: three balls of black • 3- or 4-ply/fingering yarn with a metallic finish: one ball of gold • 4mm/US 6 knitting needles or size needed to obtain the correct tension • two gold star buttons • suitable tapestry needle.

STITCHES USED

Stocking stitch: *knit 1 row, purl 1 row*, repeat from * to *.

2/2 rib: *K2, P2*, repeat from * to *.

Decrease 1 stitch, 2 stitches from each edge (on the right side of the work): work 1 stitch, then slip 1 stitch, knit 1 stitch and pass the slipped stitch over (slip1, K1, psso). Work the rest of the row until you are 2 stitches from the end then knit 2 stitches together (K2tog).

Increase 1 stitch, 2 stitches from each edge (on the right side of the work): work 1 stitch then knit into the front and back of the next stitch. Work until you are 2 stitches from the end then knit into the front and back of the next stitch. Work the final stitch.

TENSION

One 10cm (4in) square in stocking stitch, using 4mm/US 6 needles = 19 stitches and 27 rows.

METHOD

Back: cast on 74 stitches using 4mm/US 6 needles and knit in 2/2 rib for 3cm (1¼in). Continue in stocking stitch, increasing 1 stitch at each end, 2 stitches from the edge, every fourth row, 3 times (80 stitches). Continue straight. When the piece measures 12cm (4¾in), decrease 1 stitch at each end, 2 stitches from the edges (78 stitches). Count this as row 1. Repeat this decrease on rows 9, 17, 23, 27, 29, 31, 33, 35 and 37. Cast off the remaining 60 stitches.

Right belly: cast on 24 stitches using 4mm/US 6 needles and knit in 2/2 rib for 3cm (1¼in), then continue in stocking stitch, increasing 1 stitch on the right, 2 stitches from the edge, every fourth row, 4 times (28 stitches). When the piece measures 17cm (6¾in), decrease 1 stitch on the right, 2 stitches from the edge, then every fourth row, 5 times. Cast off the remaining 22 stitches.

Left belly: work as for the right bellly but in reverse to create the mirror image.

JOINING AND FINISHING

Sew the belly halves to the back from **A** to **B**. Pick up 100 stitches on the neck from **F** to **F** passing through **A**. Knit in 2/2 rib, beginning and ending with K2, for 11cm (4¼in) and cast off all the stitches. Pick up 58 stitches on the armholes from **C** to **C**, passing through **B**. Knit in 2/2 rib, beginning and ending with K2, for 2cm (¾in) and cast off all the stitches. Sew the sides from **C** to **D** and the middle of the belly from **E** to **F** and then join the ends of the neck ribbing. Embroider 'DOG' with duplicate stitches (Swiss darning) using the gold yarn doubled and following the chart. Sew on the star buttons.

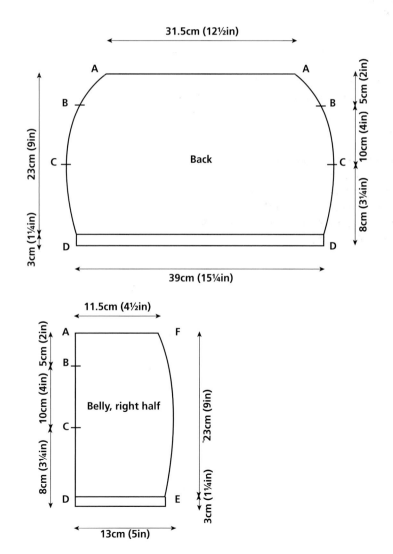

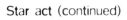

Star act (continued)

Centre stitch of the top
of the coat

Bad-boy vest

SIZE

Neck size 54cm (21¼in), chest size 66cm (26in), total back length 35cm (13¾in).

MATERIALS

Double knitting/sportweight knitting yarn in an easy-care blend: four balls of black • 3.5mm/US 4 knitting needles or size needed to obtain the correct tension • elastic thread • 190 flat-back red glass beads or rhinestones, approx. 2.4mm • one tube of textile adhesive (wash-resistant) • white tailor's chalk • paper plate • tweezers

STITCHES USED

Stocking stitch: *knit 1 row, purl 1 row*, repeat from * to *.
1/5 rib: *K1, P5*, repeat from * to *.
Garter stitch: knit every row.
Decrease 1 stitch, 2 stitches from each edge (on the right side of the work): work 1 stitch, then slip 1 stitch, knit 1 stitch and pass the slipped stitch over (slip1, K1, psso). Work the rest of the row until you are 2 stitches from the end then knit 2 stitches together (K2tog).
Increase 1 stitch, 2 stitches from each edge (on the right side of the work): work 1 stitch then knit into the front and back of the next stitch. Work until you are 2 stitches from the end then knit into the front and back of the next stitch. Work the final stitch.

TENSION

One 10cm (4in) square in 1/5 rib, using 3.5mm/ US 4 needles = 25 stitches and 30 rows.

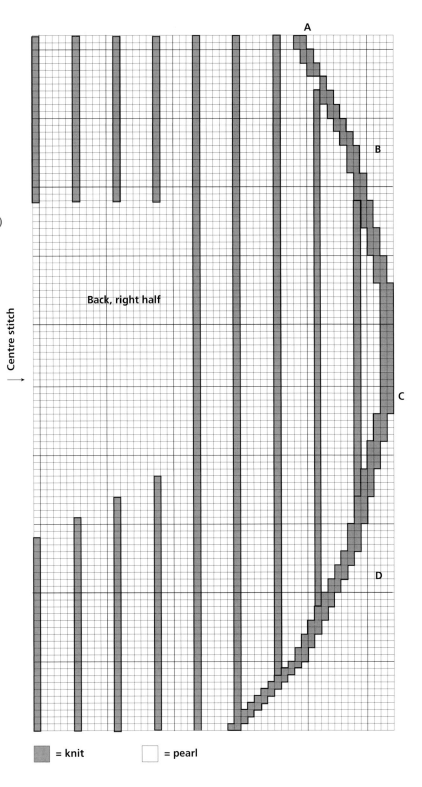

Bad-boy vest (continued)

METHOD

Back: cast on 61 stitches using 3.5mm/US 4 needles and knit in 1/5 rib following the chart, increasing and decreasing 2 stitches from each edge.

Right belly: cast on 33 stitches using 3.5mm/US 4 needles and knit in 1/5 rib following the chart on page 85, increasing and decreasing 2 stitches from the right edge.

Left belly: work as for the right belly but in reverse to create the mirror image.

Centre stitch

Back, right half

A

B

C

D

■ = knit   □ = pearl

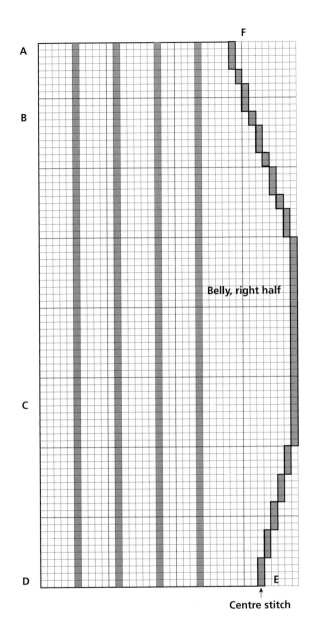

A

B

F

C

Belly, right half

D

E

Centre stitch

Method for the skull and crossbones: photocopy the skull and crossbones on page 86. Cut out the shapes. Centre the pattern on the back piece and trace the shapes of the design with the tailor's chalk. Put the adhesive on a paper plate. Pick up one lead-glass bead or rhinestone with the tweezers, dip the bottom in the adhesive and place on the contour of the design. Position the beads like this one by one, first on the contour of the skull placed 5mm (¼in) apart, then arranged over the entire surface. Leave to dry for six hours.

Tip: the layer of adhesive must be fairly thick to resist wear. The adhesive becomes completely transparent when dry.

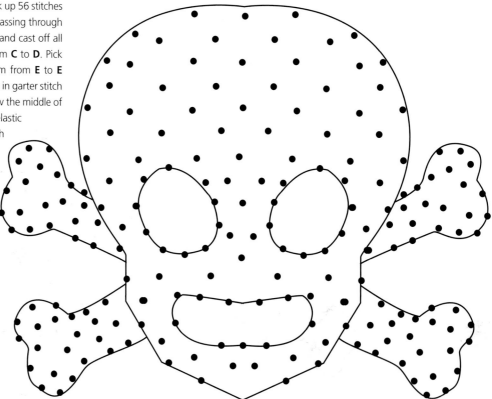

Bad-boy vest (continued)

JOINING AND FINISHING

Sew the belly halves to the back from **A** to **B**.
Pick up 158 stitches on the neck from **F** to **F**
passing through **A**. Knit 4 rows in garter stitch
and cast off all the stitches. Pick up 56 stitches
on the armholes from **C** to **C** passing through
B. Knit 4 rows in garter stitch and cast off all
the stitches. Sew the sides from **C** to **D**. Pick
up 190 stitches on the bottom from **E** to **E**
passing through **D**. Knit 4 rows in garter stitch
and cast off all the stitches. Sew the middle of
the belly from **F** to **E**. Pass an elastic
thread through the garter-stitch
rows of the neck.

Floral fancy

SIZE

Neck size 24cm (9½in), chest size 34cm (13½in), total back length 21cm (8¼in).

MATERIALS

Double knitting/sportweight cotton knitting yarn: one ball of purple • 3- or 4-ply/fingering yarn with a metallic finish: one ball of silver • 3mm/US 3 knitting needles or size needed to obtain the correct tension (see page 88) • 2mm/US B crochet hook • one stitch holder.

STITCHES USED

Half fisherman's rib: number of stitches for symmetry: multiple of 4 + 1 + 1 edge stitch at each end. **Row 1** (right side of the work): 1 edge stitch, *K2, P1, K1*, repeat from * to *, end with K1 and 1 edge stitch. **Row 2:** 1 edge stitch, P1, *K3, P1*, repeat from * to * and end with 1 edge stitch. Repeat these 2 rows.
Chain stitch.
Treble (US double) crochet.
Slip stitch.
Double (US single) crochet.

Treble (US double) cluster: wrap the yarn round the hook (yrh/yo) and insert the hook into the stitch or space – in this case into the centre hole of the chain ring – yrh/yo and draw the yarn through (3 loops on the hook). Yrh/yo and draw the yarn through the first 2 loops on the hook (2 loops on the hook). Don't complete the treble (US double) crochet stitch. Instead work two more partial trebles (US double crochets) in the same way (4 loops on the hook). Wrap the yarn round the hook and draw the yarn through all the loops.

Floral fancy (continued)

TENSION

One 10cm (4in) square in half fisherman's rib, using 3mm/US 3 needles = 32 stitches and 37 rows.

METHOD

Back: cast on 61 stitches using 3mm/US 3 needles and knit in half fisherman's rib, beginning and ending with the first stitch of the diagram for half fisherman's rib on page 89 and following the chart (right).

Belly: cast on 35 stitches using 3mm/US 3 needles and knit in half fisherman's rib, beginning and ending with the fourth stitch of the diagram for half fisherman's rib on page 89 and following the chart.

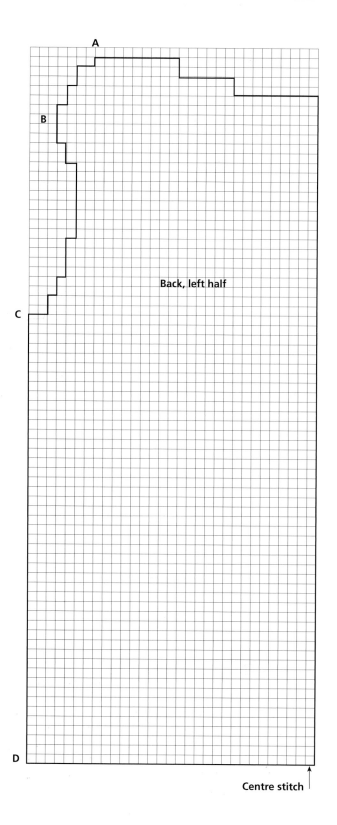

Back, left half

Centre stitch

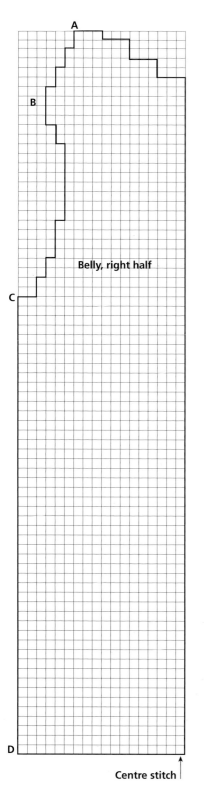

Belly, right half

A
B
C
D

Centre stitch

Flower: with the silver yarn doubled and using a 2mm/US B crochet hook, chain 4 stitches then slip stitch in the first chain to form a ring.

Round 1: chain 3 stitches; this represents the first stitch of a treble (*US double*) cluster. Working into the central hole of the chain ring, complete the treble (*US double*) cluster (you will have only 3 loops on the hook before you draw the yarn through to close the cluster). [Chain 3 stitches, work 1 treble (*US double*) cluster] 5 times, chain 3 stitches and then slip stitch into the third chain of the 3 chains at the start of the round.

Round 2: slip stitch into the next arch created by the chain of 3 stitches, chain 4 stitches, work 4 treble (*US double*) crochets into the arch, chain 3 stitches and then work 1 double (*US single*) crochet into the arch. Now [double (*US single*) crochet, chain 3, work 4 treble (*US double*) crochets, chain 3, double (*US single*) crochet all into the next arch] 5 times and slip stitch into the first chain of the 3 chains at the start of the round. Trim the yarn, leaving a tail. Weave in the yarn ends.

Crochet seven flowers.

JOINING AND FINISHING

Sew the belly to the back from **A** to **B** and from **C** to **D**. Sew six flowers around the neck, fixing them to each other with a small stitch. Sew the seventh flower at the bottom of the back on the left (see photo, page 87).

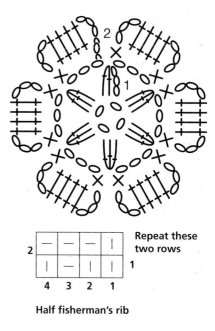

Repeat these two rows

Half fisherman's rib

⊡ = K1 on the right side; P1 on the wrong side

⊟ = P1 on the right side; K1 on the wrong side

✕ = double (*US single*) crochet

◯ = chain stitch

† = treble (*US double*) crochet

⋔ = treble (*US double*) cluster

Pretty in pink
8

SIZE

Neck size 32cm (12½in), chest size 44cm (17¼in), total back length 37cm (14½in).

MATERIALS

Aran/worsted knitting yarn in a wool blend: three balls of pink • 4mm/US 6 knitting needles or size needed to obtain the correct tension (see page 91) • one stitch holder.

STITCHES USED

Star and chevron stitches: follow the pattern.
Garter stitch: knit every row.
Increase 1 stitch on each side of the centre stitch (on the right side of the work): work until you are 1 stitch from the centre stitch then knit into the front and back of the next stitch (Kfb). Knit the centre stitch then knit into the front and back of the next stitch. Work to the end of the row.
Decrease 1 stitch on each side of the centre stitch (on the right side of the work): 2 stitches from the centre stitch, knit the 2 stitches together (K2tog), knit the centre stitch on the right side, then knit the next 2 stitches together.
Loop stitch: number of stitches for symmetry: multiple of 2 + 1 edge stitch at each end. **First row** (wrong side of the work): knit. **Second row:** 1 edge stitch, *K1, do not drop it from the left-hand needle, yarn at the front of the stitch, wrap it around the left thumb to form a loop of approximately 4cm (1½in), bring the thread round the back again, knit the stitch

from the left-hand needle again, drop the stitch from the left-hand needle, yarn over (yo) and cast off the 2 stitches on the right-hand needle on the yo, K1*. Repeat from * to * and end with 1 edge stitch. **Third row:** knit. **Fourth row:** 1 edge stitch, *K1, K1 but do not drop it from the left-hand needle, yarn at the front of the stitch, wrap it around the left thumb to form a loop of approximately 4cm (1½in), bring the thread round the back again, knit the stitch from the left-hand needle again, drop the stitch from the left-hand needle, yo and cast off the 2 stitches on the right-hand needle on the yo*. Repeat from * to * and end with 1 edge stitch.

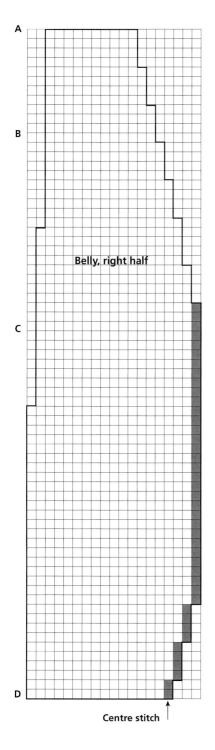

A

B

Belly, right half

C

D

Centre stitch ↑

TENSION

One 10cm (4in) square with star and chevron stitches, using 4 mm/US 6 needles = 24 stitches and 28 rows.

METHOD

Back: cast on 25 stitches using 4mm/US 6 needles and work in star and chevron stitches following the chart overleaf.

Belly: cast on 31 stitches using 4mm/US 6 needles and work in garter stitch following the chart, increasing and decreasing on each side of the centre stitch and 2 stitches from the outer edge as indicated on the chart. On row 42 cast off the centre stitch and then finish each half separately.

Neck band: cast on 50 stitches using 4mm/US 6 needles and knit 8 rows in loop stitch. Cast off all the stitches.

Pretty in pink (continued)

JOINING AND FINISHING

Pick up 63 stitches on the bottom of the back from **D** to **D** and knit 4 rows in garter stitch, i.e. 2 garter lines, and cast off all the stitches. Sew the belly to the back from **A** to **B** and from **C** to **D**, gently stretching the garter stitch of the belly. Sew the neck band around the neck.

= purl

= knit

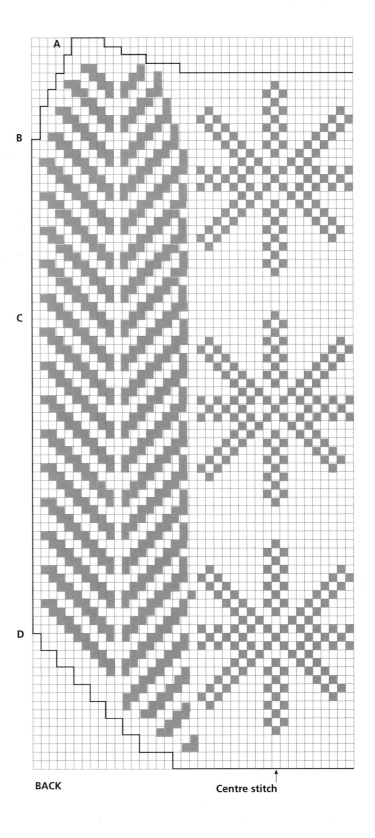

BACK

Centre stitch

Cleo all in grey

SIZE

Neck size 24cm (9½in), chest size 34cm (13½in), total back length 30cm (11¾in).

MATERIALS

Double knitting/sportweight knitting yarn in an easy-care blend: one ball of dark grey and one ball of pale grey • 3.5mm/US 4 knitting needles or size needed to obtain the correct tension.

STITCHES USED

2/2 rib: *K2, P2*, repeat from * to *.
Stocking stitch: *knit 1 row, purl 1 row*, repeat from * to *.
Striped stocking stitch: *4 dark grey rows, 4 light grey rows*, repeat from * to *.

TENSION

One 10cm (4in) striped stocking stitch square, using 3.5mm/US 4 needles = 23 stitches and 30 rows.

METHOD

Back: cast on 23 stitches in dark grey yarn using 3.5mm/US 4 needles and work in striped stocking stitch. Increase 1 stitch at each end, every second row, 16 times (55 stitches). When the piece measures 17cm (6¾in), decrease 1 stitch at each end, every fourth row, 6 times. Cast off the 43 remaining stitches. With the light grey yarn, pick up 78 stitches at the bottom of the back. Knit 4 rows in 2/2 rib, beginning and ending with K2; cast off all the stitches.

Cleo all in grey (continued)

Belly: cast on 23 stitches in dark grey yarn using 3.5mm/US 4 needles and knit 4 rows in 2/2 rib, beginning and ending with K2, then continue in striped stocking stitch. When the piece measures 6cm (2¼in), decrease 1 stitch at each end, every fourth row, 6 times. Cast off the remaining 11 stitches.

Sleeve: cast on 34 stitches in light grey yarn using 3.5mm/US 4 needles and knit 10 rows in 2/2 rib, beginning and ending with K2, then continue in stocking stitch, decreasing 1 stitch at each end, every second row, 12 times. Cast off the remaining 10 stitches. Knit a second sleeve.

JOINING AND FINISHING

Sew the sleeves to the back as well as the right sleeve to the belly from **A** to **B**. With the dark grey yarn, pick up 62 stitches all around the neck from **A** to **A**. Knit 8 rows in 2/2 rib, beginning and ending with K2 and cast off all the stitches. Sew the left sleeve to the belly from **A** to **B** and join the neck ribbing with neat stitches. Join the sides from **B** to **C** and the sleeves from **B** to **D**.

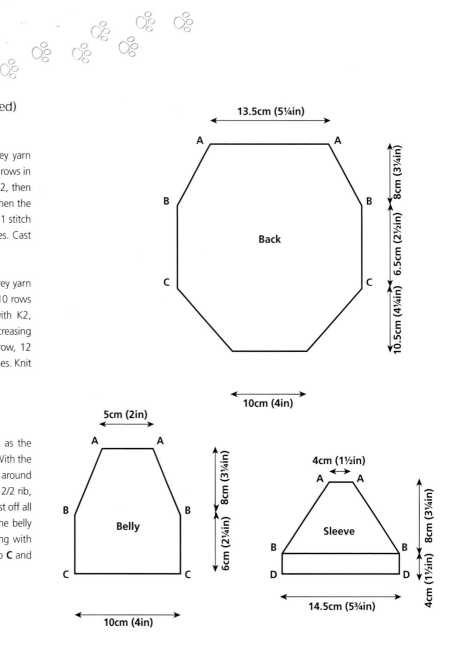

Top dog Bailey

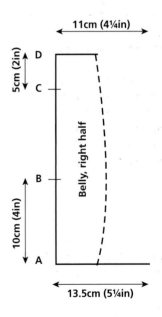

SIZE

Collar size 26cm (10¼in), chest size 36cm (14¼in), total back length 41cm (16¼in).

MATERIALS

Aran/worsted knitting yarn in an easy-care blend: two balls of black and one ball each of yellow, red, mauve and vermilion • 4mm/US 6 knitting needles or size needed to obtain the correct tension.

STITCHES USED

Striped garter stitch: knit each row. Work *4 rows black, 4 rows vermilion, 4 rows black, 4 rows red, 4 rows black, 4 rows yellow, 4 rows black, 4 rows mauve*. Repeat from * to *.

Increase 1 stitch on each side of the centre stitch (on the right side of the work): work until you are 1 stitch from the centre stitch then knit into the front and back of the next stitch (Kfb). Knit the centre stitch then knit into the front and back of the next stitch. Work to the end of the row.

Decrease 1 stitch on each side of the centre stitch (on the right side of the work): 2 stitches from the centre stitch, knit 2 stitches together (K2tog), knit the centre stitch on the right side, then K2tog.

TENSION

One 10cm (4in) square in striped garter stitch, using 4mm/US 6 needles = 20 stitches and 42 rows.

11cm (4¼in)

5cm (2in)

D

C

B

A

10cm (4in)

Belly, right half

13.5cm (5¼in)

– – – – – – = centre stitch

Top dog Bailey (continued)

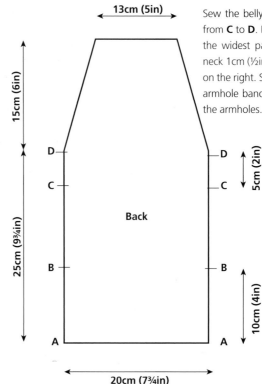

METHOD

Back beginning with the neck: cast on 40 stitches in black yarn using 4mm/US 6 needles and work in striped garter stitch. When the piece measures 25cm (9¾in), decrease 1 stitch at each end, once, then *knit 6 rows and decrease 1 stitch at each end of the sixth row, then knit 2 further rows*, repeat 3 times from * to * (26 stitches). When the piece measures 35cm (13¾in), cast off all the stitches.

Belly beginning with the neck: cast on 27 stitches in black yarn using 4mm/US 6 needles and work in striped garter stitch. When the piece measures 8cm (3¼in), increase 1 stitch on each side of the centre stitch every fourth row, twice (31 stitches). Continue straight. When the piece measures 19cm (7½in), decrease 1 stitch on each side of the centre stitch every sixth row, 4 times (23 stitches). When the piece measures 25cm (9¾in), cast off all the stitches.

Armhole bands: cast on 40 stitches in black yarn using 4mm/US 6 needles and knit 5 rows in garter stitch, i.e. 3 garter lines, and cast off all the stitches. Knit a second band.

Neck band: cast on 48 stitches in black yarn using 4mm/US 6 needles, knit 2 rows in garter stitch, then cast on 22 stitches at each end of every second row, twice, to obtain 136 stitches. Knit 8 rows, i.e. 4 garter lines, then cast off 22 stitches at each end, every second row, twice. Cast off the remaining 48 stitches in one go.

Bottom band: cast on 104 stitches in black yarn using 4mm/US 6 needles, knit 8 rows in garter stitch, i.e. 4 garter lines, and cast off all the stitches.

JOINING AND FINISHING

Sew the belly to the back from **A** to **B** and from **C** to **D**. Fold the neck band in two. Sew the widest part (the 48 stitches) on to the neck 1cm (½in) from the left and form a knot on the right. Sew the bottom band. Close the armhole bands in a round and sew them to the armholes.

13cm (5in)

15cm (6in)

D

C

Back

B

A

25cm (9¾in)

D

C

5cm (2in)

B

10cm (4in)

A

20cm (7¾in)

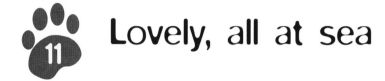

Lovely, all at sea

SIZE

Collar size 32cm (12½in), chest size 44cm (17¼in), total back length 43cm (17in).

MATERIALS

Double knitting/sportweight knitting yarn in an easy-care blend: two balls of white, one ball of navy • 3.5mm/US 4 knitting needles or size needed to obtain the correct tension • two press studs • eight gold buttons decorated with an anchor, 12mm (½in).

STITCHES USED

1/1 rib: *K1, P1*, repeat from * to *.
Striped stocking stitch: *2 rows navy, 6 rows white*, repeat from * to *.
Decrease 1 stitch (on the right side of the work): at the start of the row, knit the required number of stitches to the decrease position (2 or 9) then slip 1 stitch, knit 1 stitch and pass the slipped stitch over (slip1, K1, psso). Knit to the next decrease position (4 or 10 stitches from the end) and knit 2 stitches together (K2tog). Knit to the end.
Increase 1 stitch, 9 stitches from each edge (on the right side of the work): knit 9 stitches then knit the next 2 stitches together. Knit until you are 10 stitches from the end then knit 2 stitches together. Knit to the end.

TENSION

One 10cm (4in) square in striped stocking stitch, using 3.5mm/US 4 needles = 23 stitches and 30 rows.

METHOD

Back: cast on 61 stitches in white yarn using 3.5mm/US 4 needles and work in 1/1 rib for 6 rows, beginning with 1 edge stitch, K1 and ending with K1 and 1 edge stitch. Continue in striped stocking stitch except for the 9 stitches at each end which should be worked in 1/1 rib in white yarn. Tip: for the left ribs, prepare a small white ball and knit at the same time as the two navy rows, crossing the yarns. Increase 1 stitch at each end, 9 stitches from the edges, every second row, 9 times (79 stitches). When the piece measures 28cm (11in), that is the twelfth navy stripe, decrease 1 stitch at each end, 9 stitches from the edges, every second row, 10 times (59 stitches). Knit 8 rows in 1/1 rib and cast off all the stitches.

Lovely, all at sea (continued)

Belly: cast on 39 stitches in white yarn using 3.5mm/US 4 needles and work in 1/1 rib. When the piece measures 31cm (12¼in), cast off all the stitches.

Sleeves: cast on 68 stitches in white yarn using 3.5mm/US 4 needles and work in striped stocking stitch, beginning with 6 rows in white yarn and decreasing 1 stitch at each end, 3 stitches from the edges, every second row, 11 times (46 stitches). Continue straight and after the fourth navy stripe, knit 8 rows in 1/1 rib in white yarn and cast off all the stitches. Knit the second sleeve.

JOINING AND FINISHING

Sew the belly to the back from **B** to **C**, placing the belly under the 9 stitches of the side ribbing of the back. Sew the sleeves to the armholes under the ribbing of the back and on the belly from **A** to **B**. Sew the sleeve side seam. Sew a press stud on each side of the neck at **A**. Sew a button on to each press stud. Sew the other buttons on to the sides and the sleeves at the same time (see photo, page 31).

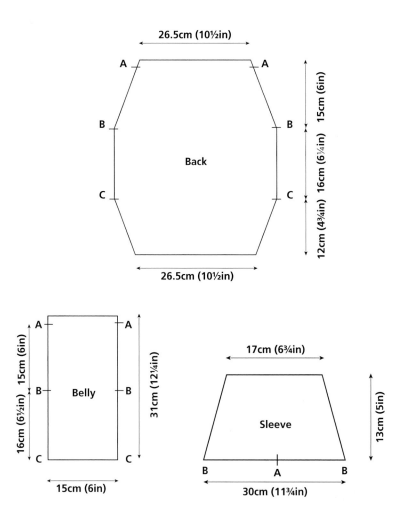

 12

Couture wear for Toto

SIZE

Collar size 54cm (21¼in), chest size 64cm (25¼in), total back length 48cm (19in).

MATERIALS

Chunky/bulky knitting yarn in an easy-care blend: five balls of scarlet • 6mm/US 10 knitting needles or size needed to obtain the correct tension • nineteen gold studs • stitch holder.

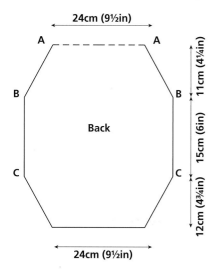

A ← 24cm (9½in) → A

B   B   11cm (4¼in)

Back   15cm (6in)

C   C   12cm (4¾in)

← 24cm (9½in) →

STITCHES USED

1/1 rib: *K1, P1*, repeat from * to *.
Diamond stitch: follow the diagram.
Decrease 1 stitch, 2 stitches from each edge (on the right side of the work): work 1 stitch, then slip 1 stitch, knit 1 stitch and pass the slipped stitch over (slip1, K1, psso). Work the rest of the row until you are 2 stitches from the end then knit 2 stitches together (K2tog).
Increase 1 stitch, 2 stitches from each edge (on the right side of the work): work 1 stitch then knit into the front and back of the next stitch. Work until you are 2 stitches from the end then knit into the front and back of the next stitch. Work the final stitch.

TENSIONS

One 10cm (4in) square in diamond stitch using 6mm/US 10 needles = 19 stitches and 22 rows. 28 stitches in 1/1 rib = 10cm (4in) and 28 stitches in stretched 1/1 rib = 20cm (7¾in).

METHOD

Back: cast on 47 stitches using 6mm/US 10 needles and knit 2 rows in 1/1 rib, beginning with 1 edge stitch, K1 and ending with K1 and 1 edge stitch. Continue in diamond stitch (see page 100), knitting 1 edge stitch, K1, followed by the boxed section 7 times, then K1 and 1 edge stitch. Increase 1 stitch at each end, 2 stitches from the edge, every second row, 12 times (71 stitches). When the piece measures 28cm (11in), i.e. 5 times the box, decrease 1 stitch at each end, 2 stitches from the edge, every second row, 10 times. Slip the remaining 51 stitches on to the stitch holder.

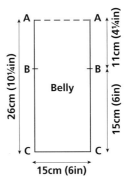

Couture wear for Toto (continued)

Belly: cast on 43 stitches using 6mm/US 10 needles and work in 1/1 rib for 26cm (10¼in), decreasing 1 stitch at each end and leaving aside the remaining 41 stitches. Note: these ribs can be stretched very easily.

JOINING AND FINISHING

Take the 51 stitches from the stitch holder, then the 41 stitches from the belly (from **A** to **A**) to obtain 92 stitches. Knit 9cm (3½in) in 1/1 rib and cast off all the stitches. Join the ends of the ribbing. Sew the sides from **B** to **C**. Fix the studs according to the stud diagram.

A - - - - A

26cm (10¼in)

B — Belly — B

11cm (4¼in)

15cm (6in)

C — C

15cm (6in)

DIAMOND STITCH

$\boxed{-}$ = P1 on the right side;
K1 on the wrong side

$\boxed{}$ = K1 on the right side;
P1 on the wrong side

Repeat the box

STUD DIAGRAM

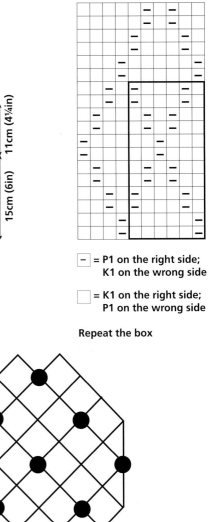

● = gold stud

Short scarf for Caramel

DIMENSIONS

80 × 17cm (31½ × 6¾in).

MATERIALS

Double knitting/sportweight knitting yarn in an easy-care blend: one ball of red and one ball of grey • 3.5mm/US 4 knitting needles or size needed to obtain the correct tension.

STITCHES USED

Open-work blanket stitch (multiple of 6 + 2 stitches). **Rows 1–2:** knit all stitches. **Row 3:** (right side of the work) K2, *cast off 4 stitches leaving the last stitch on the right-hand needle, K1*. Repeat from * to *. **Row 4:** K2, *yo, K2*. Repeat from * to *. **Row 5:** K2, *1 increase as follows: K4, taking alternately once in front, once behind the yo loop of the preceding row, K2*. Repeat from * to *. **Row 6:** knit all.

Two-coloured check with elongated stitches: follow the diagram.

Garter stitch: knit every row.

Stocking stitch: *knit 1 row (right side), purl 1 row*. Repeat from * to *.

TENSION

One 10cm (4in) square in stocking stitch, using 3.5mm/US 4 needles = 23 stitches and 30 rows.

METHOD

Cast on 74 stitches in red yarn using 3.5mm/US 4 needles and knit 6 rows in open-work blanket stitch. 52 stitches remain. Knit 2 rows in red yarn, then continue in two-coloured check, working the first 3 and last 3 stitches in garter stitch. Repeat the 8 rows of check stitch 3 times and continue with the red yarn after the 3 garter stitches with *K2, slip 1, K1, pass slipped stitch over*, repeat from * to *. Two rows higher, *K1, slip 1, K1, pass slipped stitch over*, repeat from * to *. 28 stitches remain. Now work in stocking stitch. When the piece measures 38cm (15in), cast off all the stitches. Knit a second identical band. Join the two parts of the scarf by grafting (kitchener stitch).

	= K1 on the right side, P1 on the wrong side in red yarn
	= K1 on the right side, P1 on the wrong side in grey yarn
V	= slip stitch purlwise on the right side (yarn back of stitch) or purlwise on the wrong side (yarn front of stitch) for 4 rows

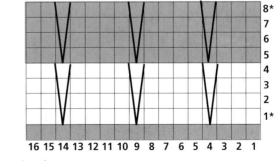

red

grey

red

8*
7
6
5
4
3
2
1*

16 15 14 13 12 11 10 9 8 7 6 5 4 3 2 1

Repeat from * to *

Long scarf and legwarmers

DIMENSIONS

Scarf: 80 × 17 cm (31½ × 6¾in).
Leg warmers: 18 × 6cm (7 x 2¼in).

MATERIALS

Double knitting/sportweight knitting yarn in an easy-care blend: three balls of mauve • 3mm/US 3 knitting needles or size needed to obtain the correct tension.

│	=	K1 on the right side or P1 on the wrong side
─	=	P1 on the right side or K1 on the wrong side
⟨X⟩	=	3 left cross stitches
⟨X⟩	=	3 right cross stitches
⟨X⟩	=	4 left cross stitches

STITCHES USED

2/2 rib: *K2, P2*, repeat from * to *.
3 left cross stitches (K2 and P1): slip 2 stitches to a cable needle in front, purl the next stitch, then knit the 2 stitches on the cable needle.
3 right cross stitches (P1 and K2): slip 1 stitch to a cable needle at the back, knit the next 2 stitches, then purl the stitch on the cable needle.
4 left cross stitches (K2 and K2): slip 2 stitches to a cable needle in front, knit the next 2 stitches, then knit the 2 stitches on the cable needle.
Crossed cables: follow the diagram.

TENSION

One 10cm (4in) square in crossed cables, using 3mm/US 3 needles = 34 stitches and 34 rows.

METHOD FOR SCARF

Cast on 56 stitches using 3mm/US 3 needles and knit 4cm (1½in) in 2/2 rib, beginning and ending with K3, then continue in crossed cables. After the twenty-third cable motif, knit 4cm (1½in) in 2/2 rib and cast off all the stitches.

METHOD FOR THE LEGWARMERS

Cast on 42 stitches using 3mm/US 3 needles and knit 3cm (1¼in) in 2/2 rib, beginning and ending with K2, then continue in crossed cables. After the fifth cable motif, knit 3cm (1¼in) in 2/2 rib and cast off all the stitches. Knit a second leg warmer. Sew the leg seam in neat backstitch.

CROSSED CABLES

Repeat from * to *

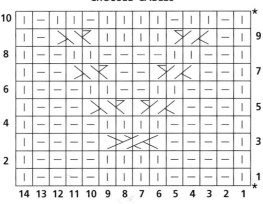

Row labels (left): 10, 8, 6, 4, 2
Row labels (right): 9, 7, 5, 3, 1
Column labels (bottom): 14 13 12 11 10 9 8 7 6 5 4 3 2 1

Seventies style for Lovely

DIMENSIONS

68 × 68cm (26¾ × 26¾in).

MATERIALS

Aran/worsted knitting yarn: four balls of black, one ball each of moss, purple, brown, blue-green, yellow, red and grey • 3.5mm/US E crochet hook.

STITCHES USED

Chain stitch, slip stitch, treble (*US double*) crochet, double (*US single*) crochet.

SQUARE

Using the centre colour, chain 4 stitches then slip stitch in the first chain to form a ring.

Round 1: chain 3 stitches for 1 treble (*US double*) crochet then chain 2 more stitches. [Working into the central hole of the chain ring, work 3 treble (*US double*) crochets, chain 2] 3 times, work 2 treble (*US double*) crochets and slip stitch into the third chain at the start of the round. Cut the yarn, leaving a tail.

Round 2: with the second colour, slip stitch into the first 2-chain arch of round 1, chain 3 stitches for 1 treble (*US double*) crochet, chain 2 stitches and work 3 treble (*US double*) crochets, all still in the first 2-chain arch of the previous round, chain 1. Add a corner motif as follows: into the next 2-chain arch work 3 treble (*US double*) crochets, chain 2, 3 treble (*US double*) crochets. [Chain 1, 1 corner motif] twice more, chain 1, 2 treble (*US double*) crochets then slip stitch into the third chain at the start of the round. Cut the yarn, leaving a tail.

Seventies style for Lovely (continued)

Round 3: with the third colour, slip stitch into the first 2-chain arch of round 2, chain 3 stitches for 1 treble (*US double*) crochet, chain 2 stitches and work 3 treble (*US double*) crochets, all still in the first 2-chain arch of the previous round, chain 1. Add a side motif as follows: into the next 2-chain arch work 3 treble (*US double*) crochets. [Chain 1, 1 corner motif (see round 2), chain 1, 1 side motif] twice more, chain 1, 2 treble (*US double*) crochets then slip stitch into the third chain at the start of the round. Cut the yarn, leaving a tail.

Round 4: using black yarn, slip stitch into the first 2-chain arch of round 3, chain 3 stitches for 1 treble (*US double*) crochet, chain 2 stitches and work 3 treble (*US double*) crochets, all still in the first 2-chain arch of the previous round, chain 1. [1 side motif, chain 1, 1 side motif, chain 1, 1 corner motif, chain 1] 3 times, 1 side motif, chain 1, 1 side motif, chain 1, 2 treble (*US double*) crochets and slip stitch into the third chain at the start of the round. Cut the yarn, leaving a tail. Weave in all the ends.

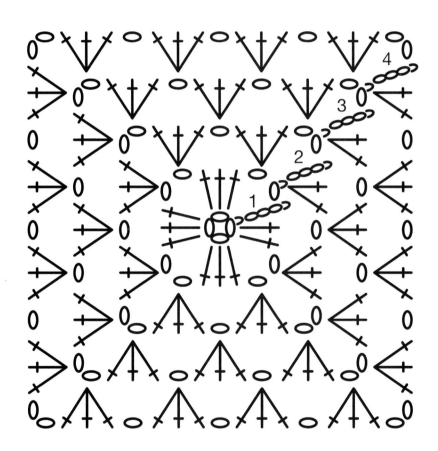

O = chain stitch

† = treble (*US double*) crochet

METHOD

The rug comprises 64 four-coloured squares. Crochet: (the order of the colours given below corresponds to the order of the rounds) **12 A squares:** purple, red, brown and black; **11 B squares:** moss, yellow, blue-green and black; **10 C squares:** red, moss, grey and black; **10 D squares:** grey, brown, yellow and black; **10 E squares:** brown, blue-green, moss and black; and **11 F squares:** grey, brown, yellow and black. Following the diagram, arrange the 8 squares of the first row side by side. Place the 8 squares of the second row on top, right side against right side. Join the first 2 squares with double (*US single*) crochet, working a row of stitches in black in the selvedge of the 2 squares then, without cutting the yarn, join the next 2 squares. Join the 8 squares of the 2 rows in this way. Add the other rows in the same way. End by making each perpendicular join in one go from one edge to the other.

A	B	C	D	E	F	A	B
F	A	B	C	D	E	F	A
E	F	A	B	C	D	E	F
D	E	F	A	B	C	D	E
C	D	E	F	A	B	C	D
B	C	D	E	F	A	B	C
A	B	C	D	E	F	A	B
F	A	B	C	D	E	F	A

Floral scarf for Lovely

17

DIMENSIONS

66 × 17cm (26 × 6¾in).

MATERIALS

Aran/worsted knitting yarn in an easy-care blend: one ball each of black, moss, purple, brown, blue-green, yellow, red and grey • 3.5mm/US E crochet hook.

STITCHES USED

Slip stitch, chain stitch, double (*US single*) crochet, treble (*US double*) crochet.
Popcorn: work 3 treble (*US double*) crochets into a single stitch or space, take the hook out of the stitch and pass it behind the top of the first treble (*US double*) crochet. Pick up the dropped loop and pull it through. This gathers the top of the 3 stitches to create a leaf or petal shape.

DAISY

Using the centre colour, chain 4 stitches then slip stitch in the first chain to form a ring.
Round 1: chain 3 stitches for 1 treble (*US double*) crochet. Working into the central hole of the chain ring, work 2 treble (*US double*) crochets and finish as for a popcorn, [chain 3, 1 popcorn] 5 times to make a total of 6 popcorns, chain 3 stitches then slip stitch into the top of the first popcorn to join the round. Cut the yarn, leaving a tail.

Round 2: join the second colour at the end of round 1, chain 1, [2 double (*US single*) crochets, chain 1, 2 double (*US single*) crochets all into the next arch] 6 times. Slip stitch into the top of the first stitch of the round. Cut the yarn, leaving a tail.
Round 3: with black yarn chain into the 1-chain arch at the start of the round in the centre of a side then double (*US single*) crochet into each of the next two stitches. [At the corner work 3 double (*US single*) crochets into the chain arch then double (*US single*) crochet into each of the next 4 stitches] 5 times, 3 double (*US single*) crochets into the final corner and double (*US single*) crochet into each of the next 2 stitches; slip stitch into the first stitch to close the round. Cut the yarn, leaving a tail. Weave in all the ends.

HALF-DAISY

Using the centre colour, chain 4 stitches then slip stitch in the first chain to form a ring.

Row 1: chain 3 stitches for 1 treble (*US double*) crochet. Working into the central hole of the chain ring, work 2 treble (*US double*) crochets and finish as for a popcorn, [chain 3, 1 popcorn] twice to make a total of 3 popcorns. Do not close into a ring. Secure the yarn end and trim it, leaving a tail.

Row 2: with the second colour, chain into the top of the end popcorn then work [2 double (*US single*) crochets, chain 1, 2 double (*US single*) crochets] into each 3-chain arch, chain 1 and slip stitch into the top of the third popcorn. Cut the yarn, leaving a tail.

Row 3: with black yarn chain into the end of the previous row, double (*US single*) crochet into each of the next 2 stitches, 3 double (*US single*) crochets into the chain stitch, double (*US single*) crochet into each of the next 4 stitches, 3 double (*US single*) crochets into the chain stitch, double (*US single*) crochet into each of the next 2 stitches, chain 1 and slip stitch into the end of the last round to finish. Cut the yarn, leaving a tail. Weave in all the ends.

 = chain stitch

✕ = double (*US single*) crochet

= kernel

Daisy

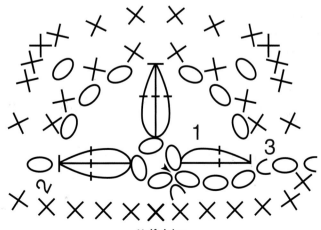

Half-daisy

Floral scarf for Lovely
(continued)

METHOD
The scarf comprises 35 daisies and 14 half-daisies. Crochet (the order of the colours given below corresponds to the order of the rounds): **7 A daisies:** yellow, blue-green and black; **7 B daisies:** purple, red and black; **7 C daisies:** moss, purple and black; **7 D daisies:** grey, moss and black; **7 E daisies:** red, brown and black; **7 F half-daisies:** blue-green, purple and black; and **7 G half-daisies:** yellow, blue-green and black. Following the diagram, arrange the 3 daisies in the first row side by side. Join them together with a row of double (*US single*) crochet stitches. Arrange the 2 half-daisies and the 2 daisies in the second row side by side. Join them together with a row of double (*US single*) crochet stitches, then join the 2 rows with 1 row of double (*US single*) crochet stitches. Add the other rows in the same way.

With the black yarn, make a chain of 28 stitches. Make 2 rows of double (*US single*) crochet stitches and fasten off to make a strap. Sew the strap on the fourth row from the bottom.

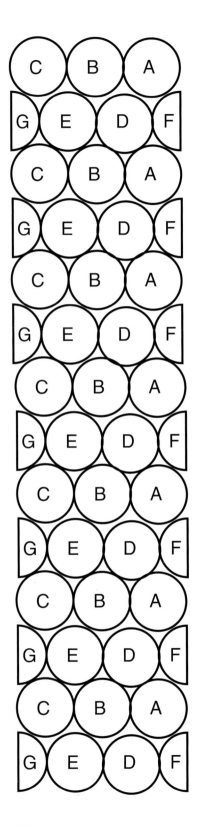

Royal cushion for Bella

DIMENSIONS

55 × 55cm (21¾ × 21¾in).

MATERIALS

Extra chunky/super bulky knitting yarn in an easy-care blend: nine balls of olive • 7mm/US 10½ and 8mm/US 11 knitting needles or size needed to obtain the correct tension • one cushion pad 55 × 55cm (21¾ × 21¾in).

STITCHES USED

Stocking stitch: *knit 1 row, purl 1 row*. Repeat from * to *.
Cherry medallion: follow the diagram.

TENSIONS

One 10cm (4in) square in stocking stitch, using 7mm/US 10½ needles = 11 stitches and 16 rows; 10cm (4in) cherry medallions = 13 stitches and 15 rows.

METHOD

Front and back: cast on 75 stitches using 8mm/US 11 needles. Work 1 edge stitch purlwise, the 19 stitches in the diagram on page 110, then from the second to the nineteenth stitch 3 times and end with 1 edge stitch purlwise. Repeat the 28 rows in the diagram 3 times to obtain a square with sides measuring approximately 55cm (21¾in). Take the 7mm/US 10½ needles and continue in stocking stitch, distributing 15 decreases on the first row. Cast off when the piece measures 110cm (43¼in) in length.

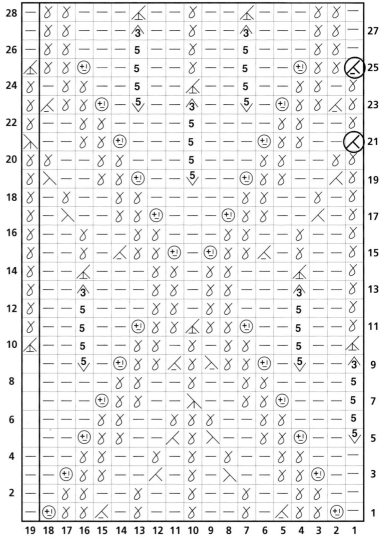

CHERRY MEDALLION

Royal cusion for Bella (continued)

JOINING AND FINISHING

Fold the knitting in half with right sides facing and sew up the sides and bottom, leaving a gap. Turn over. Slide the cushion pad inside. Sew up the gap. Cut a strip of strong card, 20cm (7¾in) wide. Roll the yarn around it 20 times to make 4 large tassels. Sew 1 tassel firmly to each corner of the cushion.

- ⊟ = P1 on the right side or K1 on the wrong side

- ⊠ = slip 1, K1, pass slipped stitch over

- ⟋ = K2tog

- ⟋ = P2tog

- ୪ = 1 stitch twisted knitwise (K1 on the right side, P1 on the wrong side)

- ⊕ = increase 1 on the wrong side: yarn in front, pick up the yarn stretched between the stitch on the right-hand needle and stitch on the left-hand needle and knit purlwise

- ↓5 = work 5 stitches into 1 knit stitch, 1 yo, K1, 1 yo and K1

- ⟋3̂ = slip 1, K1, pass slipped stitch over, K1, K2tog (= 5 stitches reduced to 2)

- ⟁ = P3tog

- 5 = K5 on the right side, P5 on the wrong side

Note

⟍ Row 21 = to be worked after the edge stitch, otherwise within the knitting during repetition of motifs, slip 1, K2tog, pass slipped stitch over (stitch 19)

⟋ Row 25 = to be worked after the edge stitch, otherwise within the knitting during repetition of motifs, P3tog (stitch 19)

Pablo loves the rain

MATERIALS

50cm (19¾in) red oilcloth, 140cm (55in) wide • 50cm (19¾in) navy blue tartan material, 140cm (55in) wide (for the lining) • 50cm (19¾in) flannelette, 140cm (55in) wide • 3m (118in) tartan bias braid, 2.5cm (1in) wide • 15cm (6in) black adhesive Velcro strip, 3cm (1¼in) wide • tacking thread • red sewing thread • pins • needles • scissors • sewing machine.

METHOD

1. Measure the size of the dog starting from the base of the neck (where the collar sits naturally) to the start of the tail: 36cm (14¼in) for Charlie and 40cm (15¾in) for Pablo.
2. Enlarge the coat pattern (see page 112) with a photocopier to adapt it to the dog's measurements and cut out.
3. Place the pattern on the wrong side of the tartan material, hold in place with pins and cut out following the pattern.
4. Place the pattern on the flannelette and cut out just like the lining. Repeat for the oilcloth.
5. For the fastening flap, cut two rectangles 25 × 10cm (9¾ × 4in) from the oilcloth and tartan fabrics.

Pablo loves the rain (continued)

6. Place the fabrics one on top of the other: the outer fabric, the flannelette, then the lining. The two outer fabrics should be right side out. Hold them together with pins, then tack all around, 1cm (½in) from the edge.

7. For the fastening flap, place the two fabric rectangles one on top of the other, sew 0.5cm (¼in) from the edges on three sides and tack the fourth small side on to the coat as shown on the pattern.

8. Machine all the layers of the coat around the edge. Remove the tacking.

9. Place the bias braid on the edge of the coat and tack where necessary, then machine. Remove the tacking.

10. Arrange the Velcro strips as shown in the diagram and sew in place.

TIP

Oilcloth is very easy to maintain but keep it rolled around a pole (or flat) as, once folded, it is difficult to recover its smooth appearance.

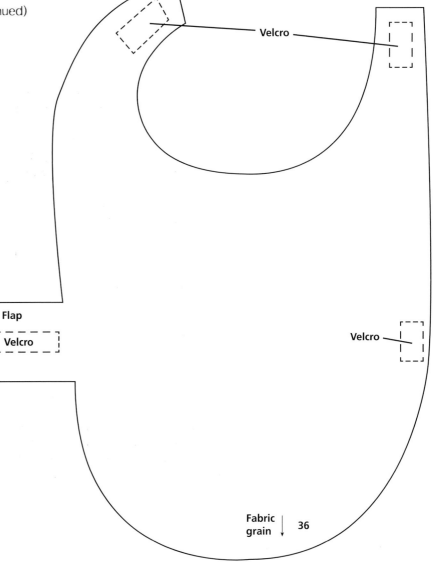

Velcro

Flap

Velcro

Velcro

Velcro

Fabric grain 36

Twice as nice reversible coat

MATERIALS

50cm (19¾in) black-and-white check material, 140cm (55in) wide • 50cm (19¾in) white spotted material on a black background, 140cm (55in) wide (for the lining) • 50cm (19¾in) flannelette, 140cm (55in) wide • 3m (118in) black satin bias braid, 2.5cm (1in) wide • 15cm (6in) black adhesive Velcro strip, 3cm (1¼in) wide • tacking thread • black sewing thread • pins • needles • scissors • sewing machine.

METHOD

1. Measure the size of the dog starting from the base of the neck (where the collar sits naturally) to the start of the tail: 36cm (14¼in) for Charlie and 40cm (15¾in) for Pablo.

2. Enlarge the coat pattern (see page 112) with a photocopier to adapt it to the dog's measurements and cut out.

3. Place the pattern on the wrong side of the check material, hold in place with pins and cut out following the pattern.

4. Place the pattern on the flannelette and cut out just like the check fabric. Repeat for the spotted fabric.

5. For the fastening flap, cut two rectangles 25 × 10cm (9¾ × 4in) from the two black-and-white materials.

6. Place the fabrics one on top of the other: the outer fabric, the flannelette, then the lining. The two outer fabrics should be right side out. Hold them together with pins, then tack all around, 1cm (½in) from the edge.

7. For the fastening flap, place the two fabric rectangles one on top of the other, sew 0.5cm (¼in) from the edges on three sides and tack the fourth small side on to the coat as shown on the pattern.

8. Machine all the layers of the coat around the edge. Remove the tacking.

9. Place the bias braid on the edge of the coat and tack where necessary, then machine. Remove the tacking.

10. Arrange the Velcro strips as shown in the diagram and sew (see diagram opposite).

Charlie lords it up

21

MATERIALS

50cm (19¾in) red tartan fabric, 140cm (55in) wide • 50cm (19¾in) navy blue tartan fabric, 140cm (55in) wide (for the lining) • 50cm (19¾in) flannelette, 140cm (55in) wide • 3m (118in) red satin bias braid, 2.5cm (1in) wide • 15cm (6in) black adhesive Velcro strip, 3cm (1¼in) wide • tacking thread • red sewing thread • pins • needles • scissors • sewing machine.

METHOD

1. Measure the size of the dog starting from the base of the neck (where the collar sits naturally) to the start of the tail: 36cm (14¼in) for Charlie and 40cm (15¾in) for Pablo.

2. Enlarge the coat pattern with a photocopier to adapt it to the dog's measurements and cut out.

3. Place the pattern on the wrong side of each tartan fabric, hold in place with pins and cut out following the pattern.

4. Place the pattern on the flannelette and cut out in the same way.

5. For the fastening flap, cut two rectangles 25 × 10cm (9¾ × 4in) from the two tartan fabrics.

6. Place the fabrics one on top of the other: the outer fabric, the flannelette, then the lining. The two outer fabrics should be right side out. Hold them together with pins, then tack all around, 1cm (½in) from the edge.

7. For the fastening flap, place the two fabric rectangles one on top of the other, sew together 0.5cm (¼in) from the edges on three sides and tack the fourth small side on to the coat as shown on the pattern.

8. Machine all the layers of the coat around the edge. Remove the tacking.

9. Place the bias braid on the edge of the coat and tack where necessary, then machine. Remove the tacking.

10. Arrange the Velcro strips as shown in the diagram and sew in place.

TIPS

Before sewing, wash the tartan fabrics
and flannelette to preshrink them. Choose
washable fabrics (check the labels).
The adhesive Velcro makes fitting easier
but sew it on otherwise it comes off.

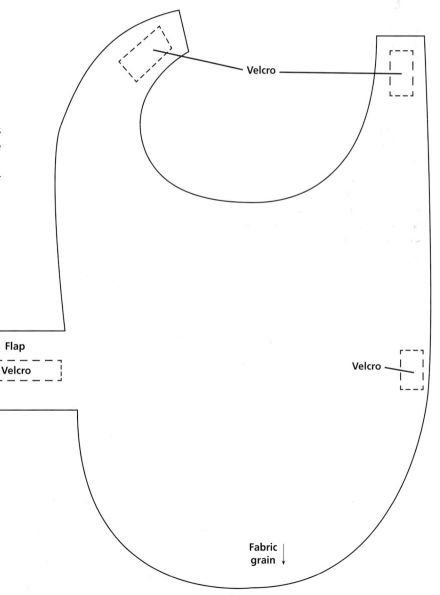

Velcro

Velcro

Flap

Velcro

Velcro

Fabric grain

So chic

22

SIZE

80 x 80cm (31½ x 31½in) tartan rug.

MATERIALS

80cm (31½in) red tartan fabric, 140cm (55in) wide • 80cm (31½in) navy blue tartan fabric, 140cm (55in) wide • 80cm (31½in) red cotton fabric, 140cm (55in) wide • 80cm (31½in) flannelette, 140cm (55in) wide • 50cm (20in) white polar fleece, 140cm (55in) wide • 1m (39¼in) fusible web, e.g. Bondaweb or Steam-A-Seam at least 40cm (15¾in) wide • navy blue sewing thread • tacking thread • pins • needles • tape measure • tailor's chalk • scissors • sewing machine.

METHOD

1. Cut an 80cm (31½in) square in the red tartan fabric, flannelette and red fabric.
Cut four strips, 95 × 10cm (37½ × 4in), in the navy blue tartan fabric.
Cut four strips, 80 × 4.5cm (31½ × 1¾in), in the polar fleece.

2. Enlarge the motif of the dog to the required dimensions and trace it on to the paper side of the fusible web. Cut it out roughly.

3. Place the navy blue tartan fabric right side down and put the roughly cut webbing rough side down on top. Iron the paper side without steam on the 'wool' position. Cut out the dog motif neatly.

4. Make a slight tear in the paper with a pin and remove.

5. Place the dog on the polar fleece, hold in place with pins, if necessary, and iron to fuse in place. Cut out the polar fleece all around leaving 0.5cm (¼in) surplus.

6. Fuse more webbing to the polar fleece on the back of the dog then trim the excess and remove the paper film. Place all this in the middle of the red tartan square and iron to fuse in place.

7. Lay out the red square with the flannelette on top and the tartan fabric with the dog on top of that. Tack the perimeter 2cm (¾in) from the edges to hold all the layers together.

8. Sew the contour of the dog template using zigzag stitch following the edge of the navy blue tartan fabric.

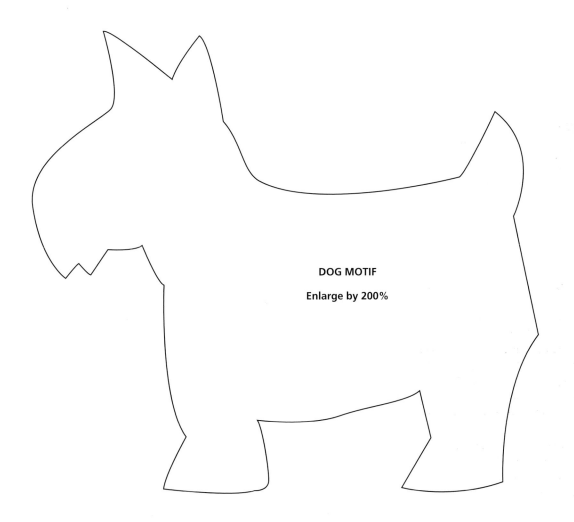

DOG MOTIF

Enlarge by 200%

9. Machine all round the tartan rug 2cm (¾in) from the edges.

10. To obtain a strip approximately 3.3m × 10cm (130 × 4in) wide, place two strips of navy blue tartan fabric in a right angle and sew diagonally. Do the same with the third strip and finally the fourth.

11. Fold this strip in two back to back lengthwise and fold again over the entire length, 1cm (¼in) of each side back to back, to obtain a width of 4cm (1½in).

12. Place this strip of fabric over the edge of the tartan rug and secure with pins.

13. On each side, under the navy blue tartan strip, slide in a strip of polar fleece, allowing it to go over by 0.5cm (¼in) and tack as you go. Then machine all the layers. Remove the tacking stitches.

TIPS

Choose washable fabrics.
Before sewing, wash all the fabrics and the polar fleece.
Fusible webbing is very fine and the best thing to use to bond the fabrics.
Zigzag stitch holds all the fabric layers together firmly.

Haute couture lead and collar

SIZE

For a collar 32cm (12½in) minimum and 52cm (20½in) maximum and a lead approximately 95cm (37½in) long.

MATERIALS

125cm (49¼in) white strap, 2.5cm (1in) wide • 125cm (49¼in) fusible web, e.g. Bondaweb or Steam-A-Seam at least 40cm (15¾in) wide • 15cm (6in) Chanel-style fabric, 140cm (55in) wide • one gold swivel trigger hook, 2.5cm (1in) wide (lead) • one side-release buckle (to fasten the collar): one male and one female part, 2.5cm (1in) wide • sliplock ring, 2.5cm (1in) wide • one brass D-ring, 2.5cm (1in) wide • one large bead with a small ring • One 3cm (1¼in) gold jump ring or split ring • sewing thread • scissors • iron • sewing machine.

METHOD

1. Cut a rectangle 15 × 125cm (6 × 49¼in) in the fusible web.
2. Place the rough side on the wrong side of the fabric and iron the paper surface with a hot (steam-free) iron.
3. Cut a strip 6 × 65cm (2¼ × 25½in) for the collar and a second strip 6 × 125cm (2¼ × 49¼in) for the lead.

The lead

4. After removing the paper film, place the strap in the middle of the strip measuring 6 × 125cm (2¼ × 49¼in). Fold the fabric in three on the strap and iron the two sides of the lead with a hot (steam-free) iron until the fabric sticks firm.
5. Sew the middle of the strip in feather stitch to prevent the fabric from fraying.

6. For the wrist loop, fold one of the ends at 20cm (7¾in) and sew two lines of tight zigzag stitch widthways, close to the join.
7. At the other end, fold at 5cm (2in), over the swivel trigger hook and sew two lines of tight zigzag stitch widthways, all along the edge to secure it.

The collar

8. After removing the paper film from the 6 × 65cm (2¼ × 25½in) strip, fold the strip in three to obtain a width of 2.5cm (1in) and iron the two sides with a hot (steam-free) iron until the fabric sticks firmly.

9. Sew the middle of the strip in feather stitch to prevent the fabric from fraying.

10. Fold one of the edges at 3cm (1¼in) and slip this end on to the centre bar of the sliplock ring; secure with zigzag stitch.

11. Place the second end of the strip through the male side-release buckle, then slip this end into the sliplock ring.

12. Bring out this end and fold at 5cm (2in), slip on the D-ring, then the female side-release buckle. Sew in zigzag stitch, first along the buckle, then after the D-ring, then on the end of the strip.

13. Attach the bead to the collar using the gold ring.

TIPS

Before sewing, wash the fabric with special wool detergent.

Zigzag stitch enables all the fabric layers to be held together firmly. Feather stitch is both secure and decorative.

Jewelled collar for Charlie

MATERIALS

One key ring • three small trigger hooks • one button ball plaited with gold thread • three pink scooby strings • one plastic heart • two small bells • two small medals • one small brass heart • one plastic bone • five pink and brown wooden beads • one brown felt square, 5cm (2in) in dimension • one small bright pink chain • fuchsia coloured ribbons • small rings for the costume jewellery.

Rummage in the bottom of your drawers or search in second-hand (thrift) shops for the above accessories, making sure that they have a ring so that they can be attached, or choose your own selection.

METHOD

First trigger hook: attach the chain with the bone, two bells, brass heart and small medals and knot on a ribbon.

Second trigger hook: plait the scooby strings over a length of approximately 4cm (1½in). Thread the five wooden beads on to the scooby string. Attach the beaded scooby string and plaited ball.

Third trigger hook: cut out a small dog in the felt square. Attach a knotted ribbon, the plastic heart and the cut-out dog into which a small ring has been fixed. Attach the three trigger hooks to the key ring which itself will be attached to the collar ring.

Skull and crossbones pendant for Clovis

MATERIALS

Double knitting/sportweight knitting yarn in a wool blend: one ball each of black and white • 1.75mm/US No. 0 crochet hook • needle for the embroidery • one trigger hook for each pendant.

STITCHES USED

Chain stitch, slip stitch, double (*US single*) crochet and backstitch.

METHOD

In white or black yarn chain 13 stitches.

Rows 1–5: chain 1 (turning chain) then double (*US single*) crochet into each chain (13 stitches), turn.

Row 6: slip stitch into each of the first 3 stitches then double (*US single*) crochet into each of the next 7 stitches, turn.

Rows 7–9: chain 1 (turning chain) then double (*US single*) crochet into each of the next 7 stitches, turn.

Row 10: chain 1 (turning chain), skip the first stitch, double (*US single*) crochet the next 4 stitches together then slip stitch in the next stitch. Cut the yarn, leaving a tail.

Make a second shape in the same way. Weave in the thread ends.

Overlay the 2 sides of the skull and crossbones and join with a row of double (*US single*) crochet stitches around the perimeter of the shape. Slip in a little synthetic filling before joining completely. Fix the trigger hook with 3 backstitches on the centre of the head. With the black colour on a white background or white on black background, embroider the details of the skull and crossbones in straight stitch.

 # Bone and precious pendants

MATERIALS

For the bone pendant, double knitting/ sportweight knitting yarn in an easy-care blend: one ball each of blue and white. For the precious pendant, 3- or 4-ply/fingering yarn with a metallic finish: one ball of silver • 1.75mm/US No. 0 crochet hook • synthetic filling • one trigger hook for each pendant.

STITCHES USED

Chain stitch, slip stitch, double (*US single*) crochet.

METHOD

The shape of the bone is mirrored on each side of the basic chain of 10 stitches. Do not make a chain stitch to turn on each row except on row 1.

Chain 10 stitches.
Row 1: chain 1, double (*US single*) crochet in each chain, turn (10 stitches).
Row 2: work 2 double (*US single*) crochets in the first stitch, double (*US single*) crochet in each of the next 8 stitches and then work 2 double (*US single*) crochets in the last stitch.
Row 3: double (*US single*) crochet in each of the first 3 stitches, turn.
Row 4: double (*US single*) crochet in each of the first 2 stitches. Cut the yarn, leaving a tail. On the other end of row 2 repeat rows 3 and 4 to shape the bone. Cut the yarn, leaving a tail.

On the other side of the basic chain, repeat rows 1–4. Cut the yarn, leaving a tail. The first side of the bone is complete. Make a second shape in the same way. Weave in the yarn ends.

Overlay the two sides of the bone and join with a row of double (*US single*) crochet stitches around the edge of the shape, inserting a little synthetic filling before joining completely. Fix the trigger hook to the centre top of the bone with 3 backstitches.

Little bells for Lovely

MATERIALS

Double knitting/sportweight knitting yarn in an easy-care blend: one ball each of pink, orange and pale green • 1.75mm/ US No. 0 crochet hook • synthetic filling • three trigger hooks.

STITCHES USED

Chain stitch, slip stitch, double (*US single*) crochet.

METHOD

In the main colour chain 4 stitches then slip stitch in the first chain to form a ring.

Round 1: chain 1 stitch then work 8 double (*US single*) crochet stitches into the centre hole; slip stitch into the first stitch to close the round.

Round 2: chain 1 stitch [1 double (*US single*) crochet in the next stitch, 2 double (*US single*) crochets in the following stitch] 4 times then slip stitch to close the round (12 stitches).

Rounds 3 and 4: chain 1 stitch, then double (*US single*) crochet in each stitch around; slip stitch to close the round.

Round 5: chain 1 stitch [double (*US single*) crochet in the next stitch, skip 1 stitch] 6 times; slip stitch to close the round (6 stitches).

Round 6: chain 1 stitch, work 2 double (*US single*) crochets into each stitch around; slip stitch to close the round (12 stitches).

Round 7: chain 1 stitch [1 double (*US single*) crochet in the next stitch, 2 double (*US single*) crochets in the following stitch] 6 times; slip stitch to close the round (18 stitches).

Rounds 8–10: chain 1, double (*US single*) crochet into each stitch around; slip stitch to close the round. At the end of round 10 trim the yarn, leaving a tail.

For the base: in the main colour chain 4 stitches then slip stitch into the first chain to form a ring.

Round 1: chain 1 stitch then work 8 double (*US single*) crochet stitches into the centre hole; slip stitch into the first stitch to close the round.

Round 2: chain 1 stitch [1 double (*US single*) crochet in the next stitch, 2 double (*US single*) crochets in the following stitch] 4 times then slip stitch to close the round (12 stitches).

Round 3: chain 1 stitch [1 double (*US single*) crochet in the next stitch, 2 double (*US single*) crochets in the following stitch] 6 times then slip stitch to close the round (18 stitches).

Round 4: chain 1 stitch [double (*US single*) crochet in each of the next 3 stitches, 2 double (*US single*) crochets in the following stitch] 4 times, double (*US single*) crochet in each of the next 2 stitches; slip stitch to close the round (22 stitches). Trim the yarn, leaving enough of a tail to join the two parts together.

Join the two parts with a row of double (*US single*) crochet, inserting some synthetic filling before joining completely. Embroider a few large vertical stitches in a contrasting colour, using straight stitch. Fix a trigger hook with 3 backstitches at the top of each bell. Weave in the yarn ends.

A heart for Bella

MATERIALS

Double knitting/sportweight yarn in an easy-care blend: one ball of pink • small quantity of fine black yarn or embroidery thread • 1.75mm/ US No. 0 crochet hook or size of your choice (exact gauge is not important) • suitable tapestry needle • synthetic filling • one trigger hook.

STITCHES USED

Chain stitch, slip stitch, double (*US single*) crochet stitch.

METHOD

Chain 2 stitches (the second is a turning chain).
Row 1: work 3 double (*US single*) crochets into the basic chain stitch; turn.
Row 2: chain 1 stitch, work 1 double (*US single*) crochet into the first stitch, 3 double (*US single*) crochets into the second stitch and 1 double (*US single*) crochet into the final stitch; turn (5 stitches).
Row 3: chain 1 stitch, work 1 double (*US single*) crochet into each of the first 2 stitches, 3 double (*US single*) crochets into the third stitch and one double (*US single*) crochet into each of the 2 remaining stitches; turn (7 stitches).
Row 4: chain 1 stitch, work 1 double (*US single*) crochet into each of the first 3 stitches, 3 double (*US single*) crochets into the fourth stitch and one double (*US single*) crochet into each of the 3 remaining stitches; turn (9 stitches).

Rows 5–6: chain 1 stitch then work one double (*US single*) crochet into each stitch; turn.
Work on the right part of the heart.
Row 7: chain 1 stitch then work 1 double (*US single*) crochet into each of the first 3 stitches; turn.
Row 8: chain 1 stitch then work 1 double (*US single*) crochet into each of the first 2 stitches. Trim the yarn leaving a tail.
Repeat rows 7 and 8 in reverse at the other end of row 6.
Make a second heart shape in the same way. Weave in the yarn ends.
Overlay the two sides of the heart and join them with a row of double (*US single*) crochet around the perimeter of the heart, slipping in a little synthetic filling before joining completely. Attach the trigger hook with 3 backstitches on the centre of the heart at the top. Embroider the word 'DOG' in straight stitch in black. Fix the trigger hook to the collar.

Lovely, Shih Tzu

Pablo, Border Terrier

Cleo, Chihuahua

Tinker, Jack Russell

Clovis, Yorkshire Terrier

Toby, Jack Russell

Bella, baby Chihuahua

Caramel, Shih Tzu

Charlie, dwarf Schnauzer

Bailey, dwarf Dachshund

Toto, French Bull Dog

A huge thank you to all the dogs and their owners.

Acknowledgements

Patterns by:
Marie-Noëlle Bayard
(pages 10 to 24, page 28, page 34, page 36, pages 56 to 62)

Marguerite Aténian
(page 30 and page 32)

Catherine Guerrier
(pages 42 to 54)

Nancy Waille
(page 38)

Thank you to **Sylvie Gourin** for knitting such a pretty coat for Cleo (page 26)